ANIMAL HEADS

ColoringBook

50 DESIGNS

K.S PUBLISHING HOUSE

COPYRIGHT DISCLAMER

This coloring book belongs To.

Color Test Page

Color Test Page

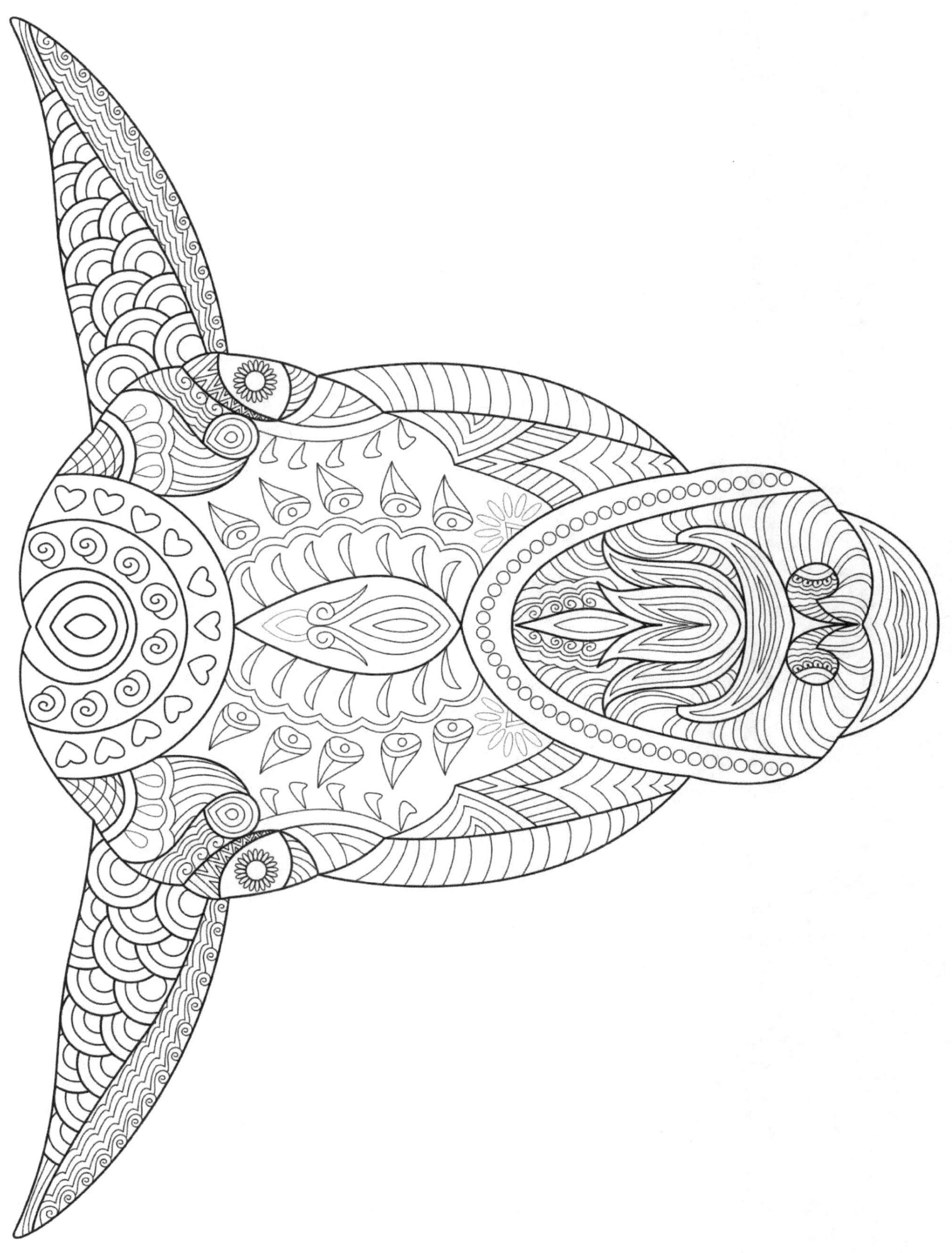

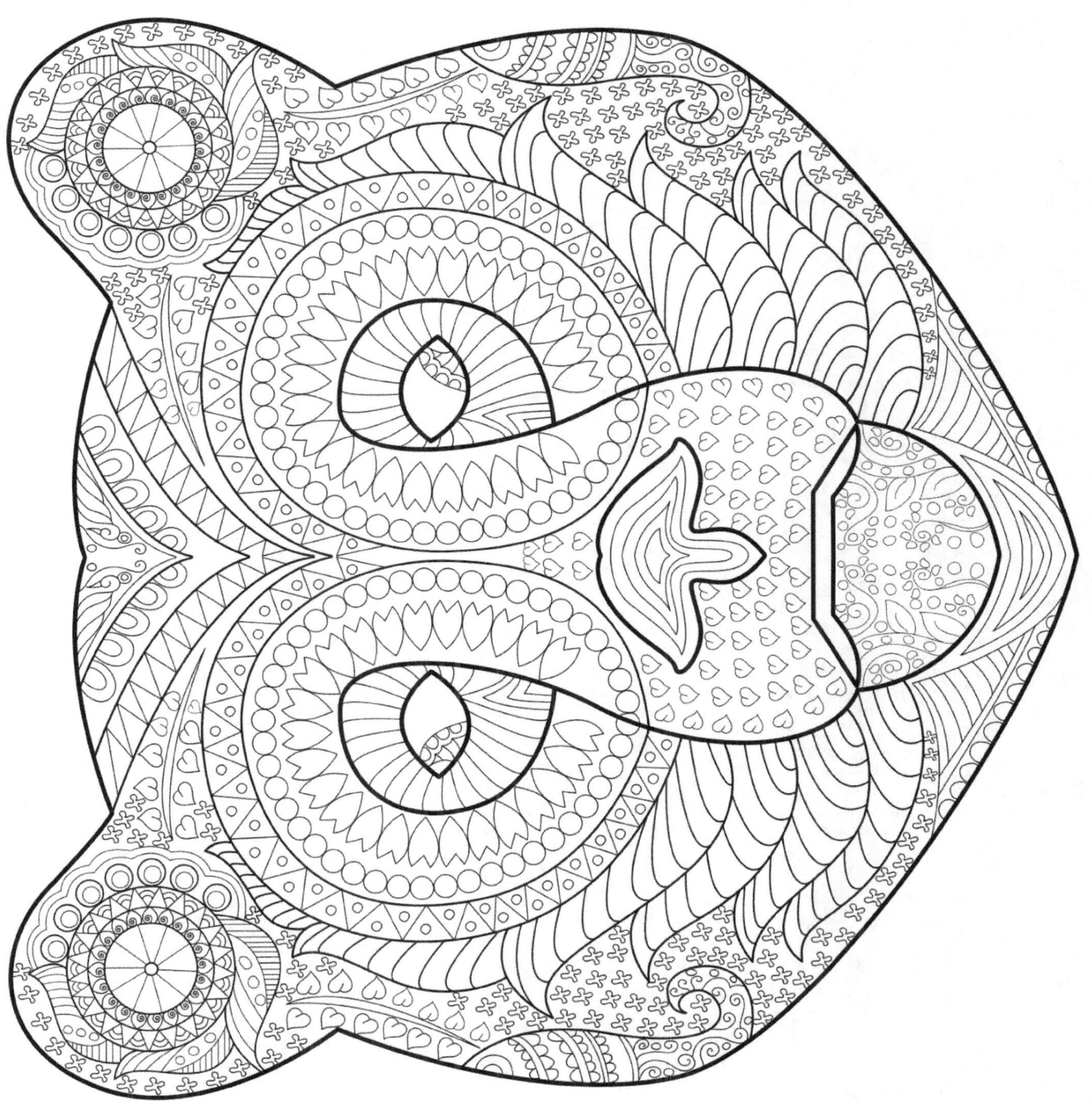

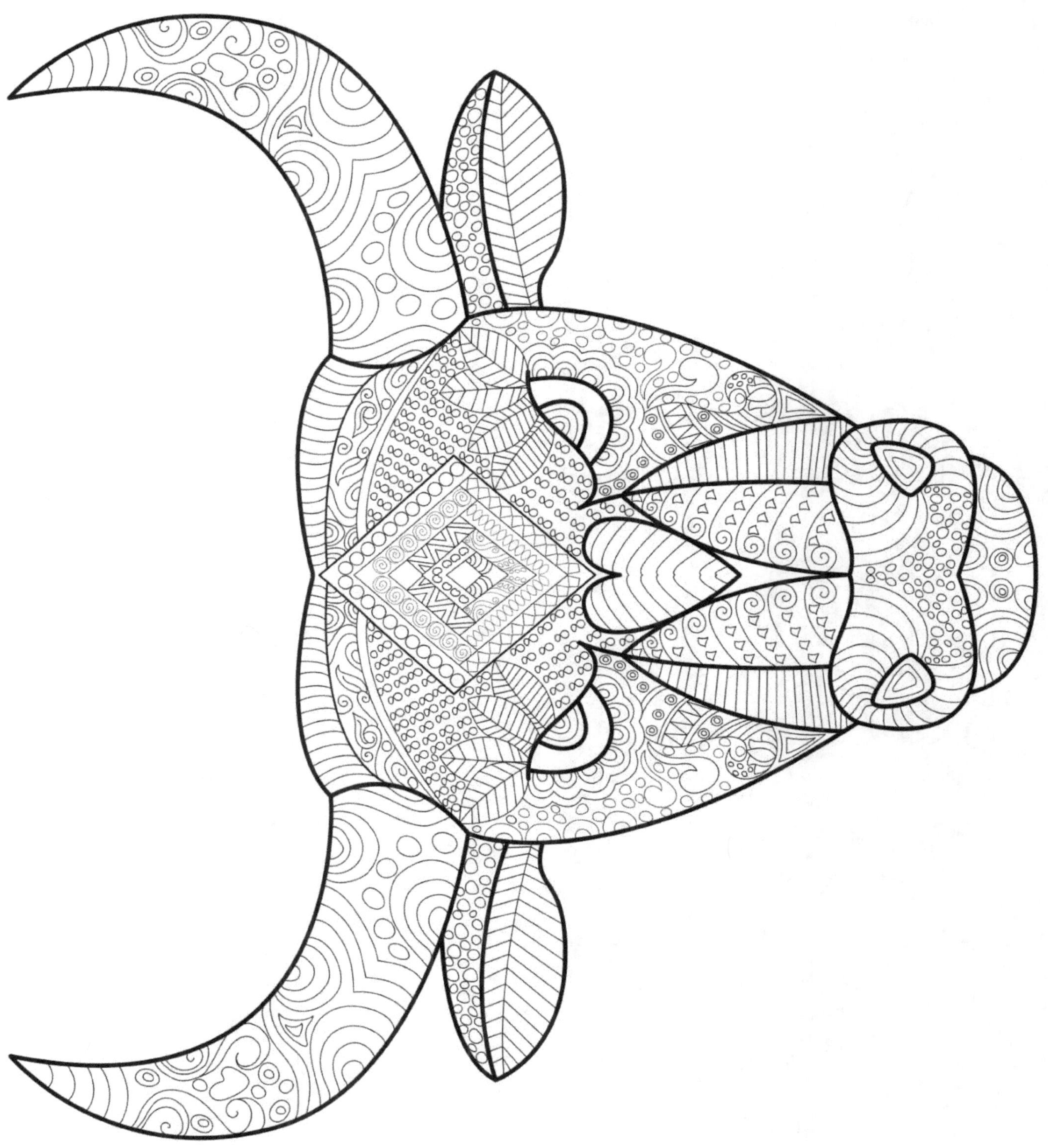

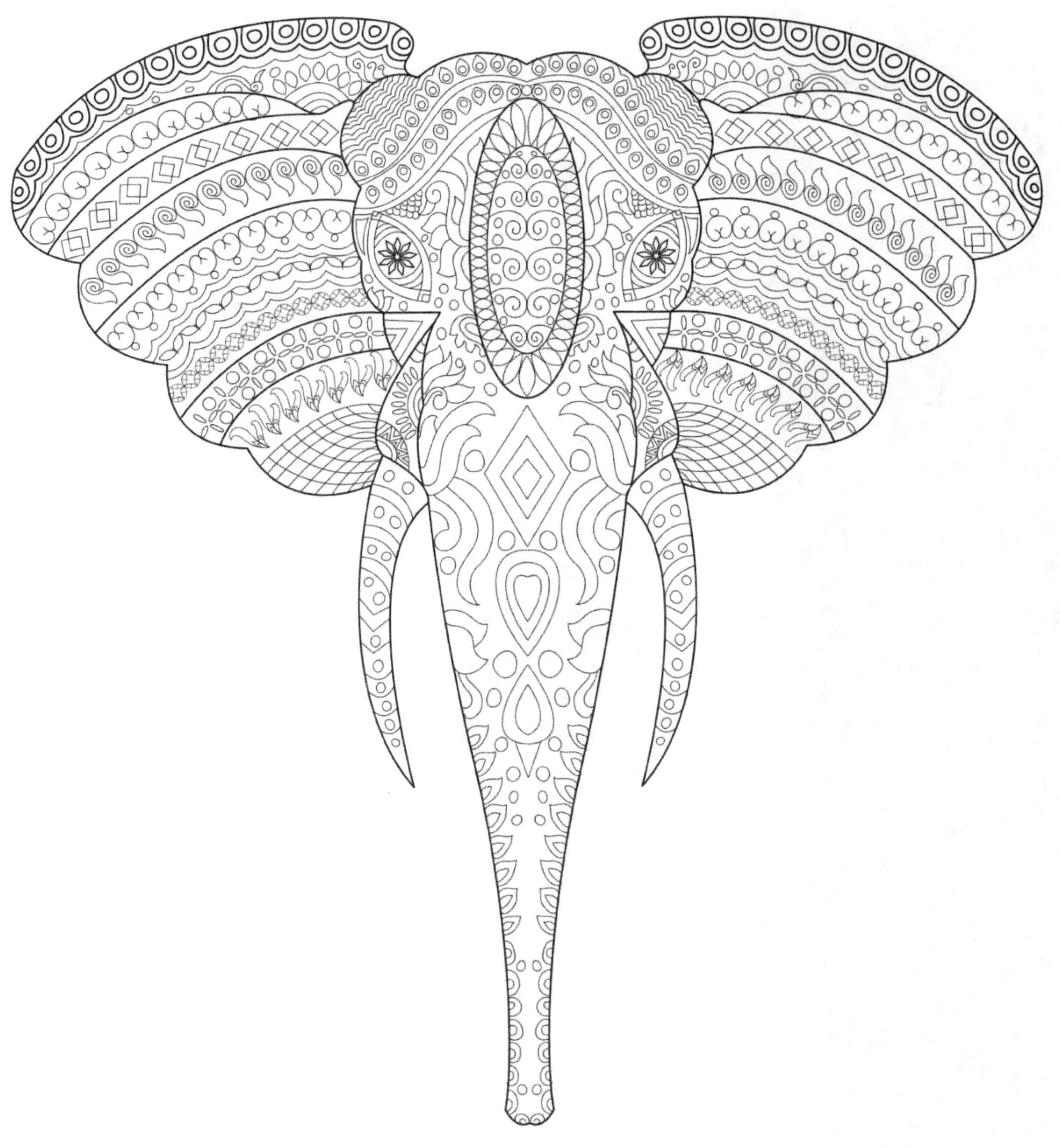

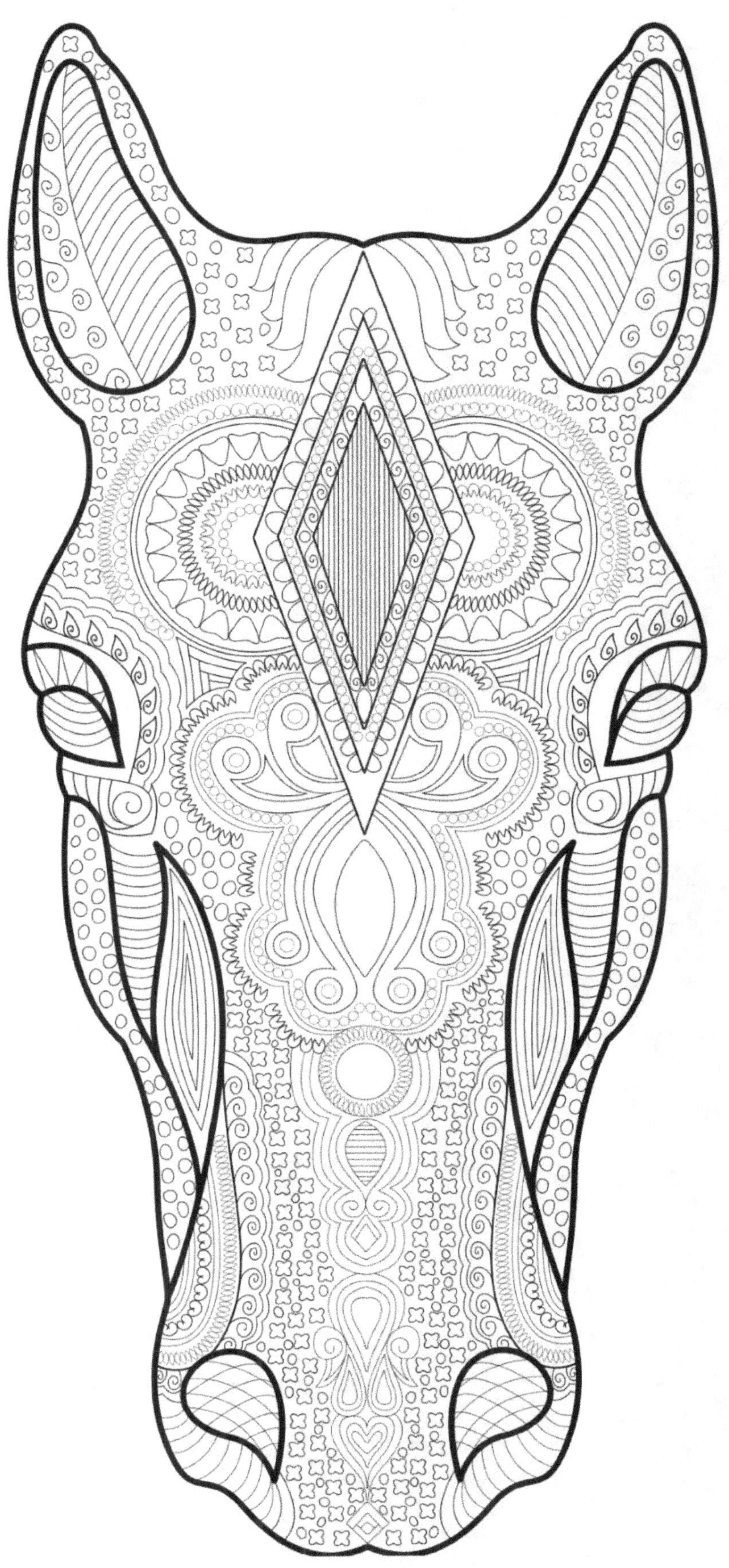

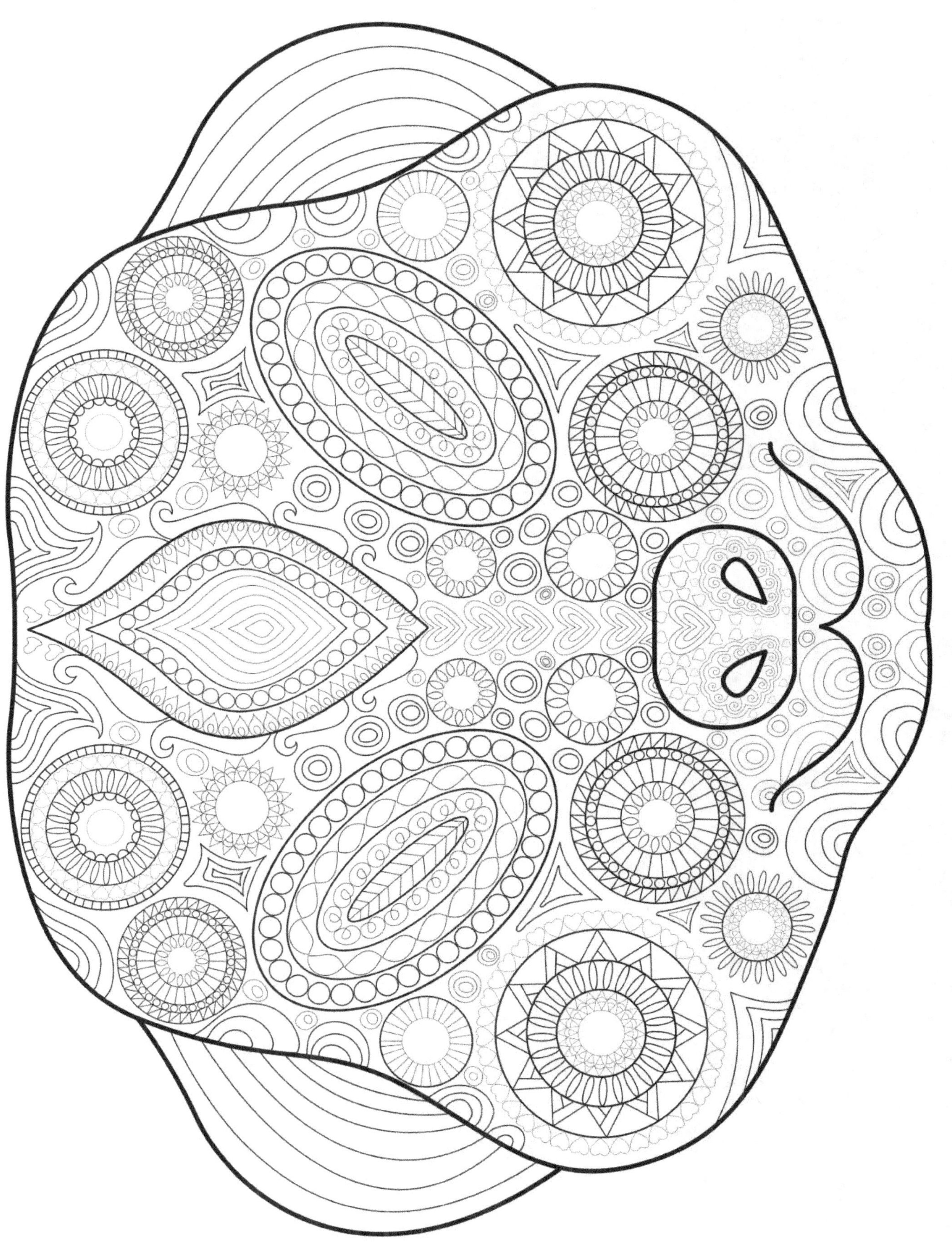

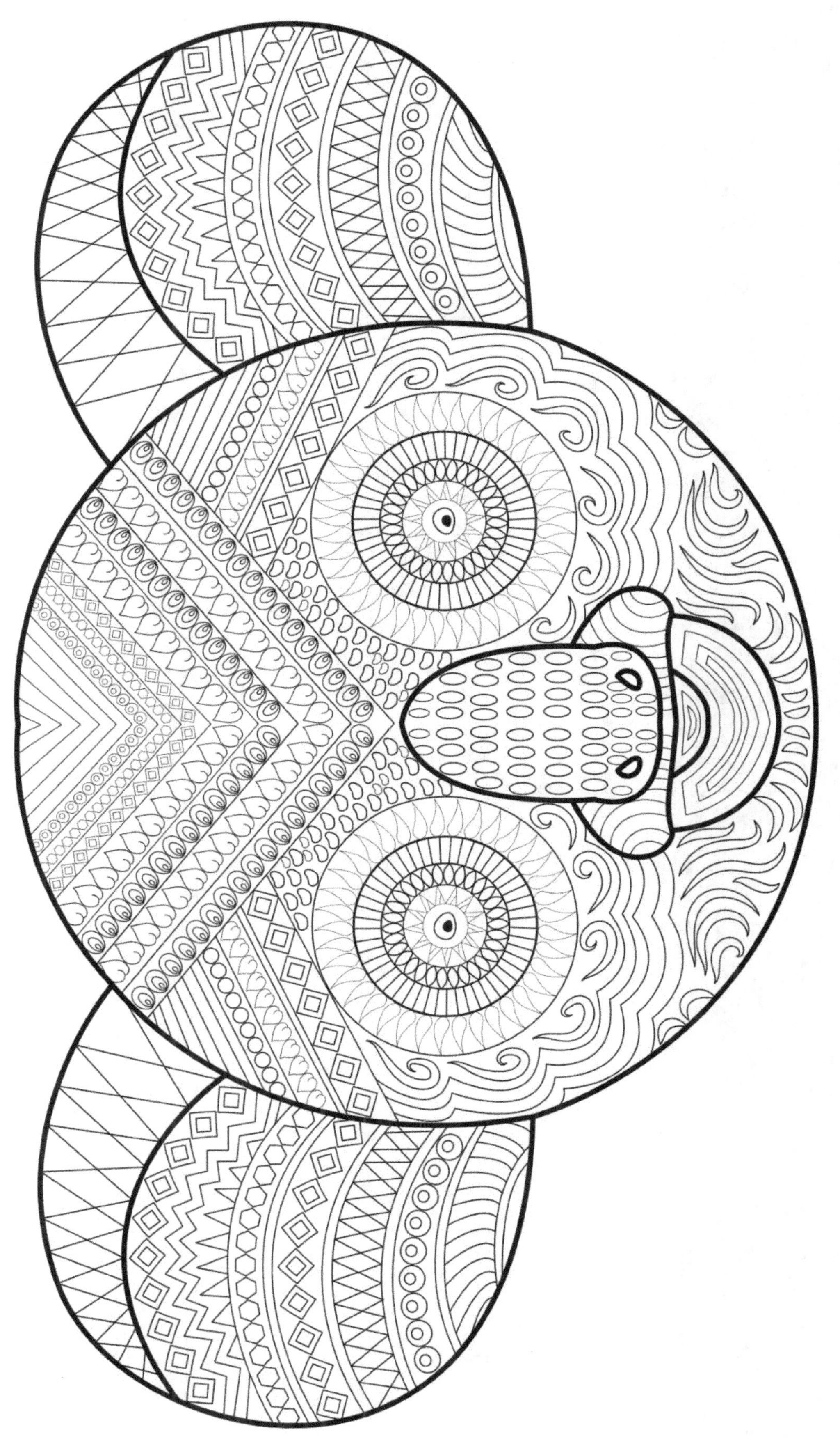

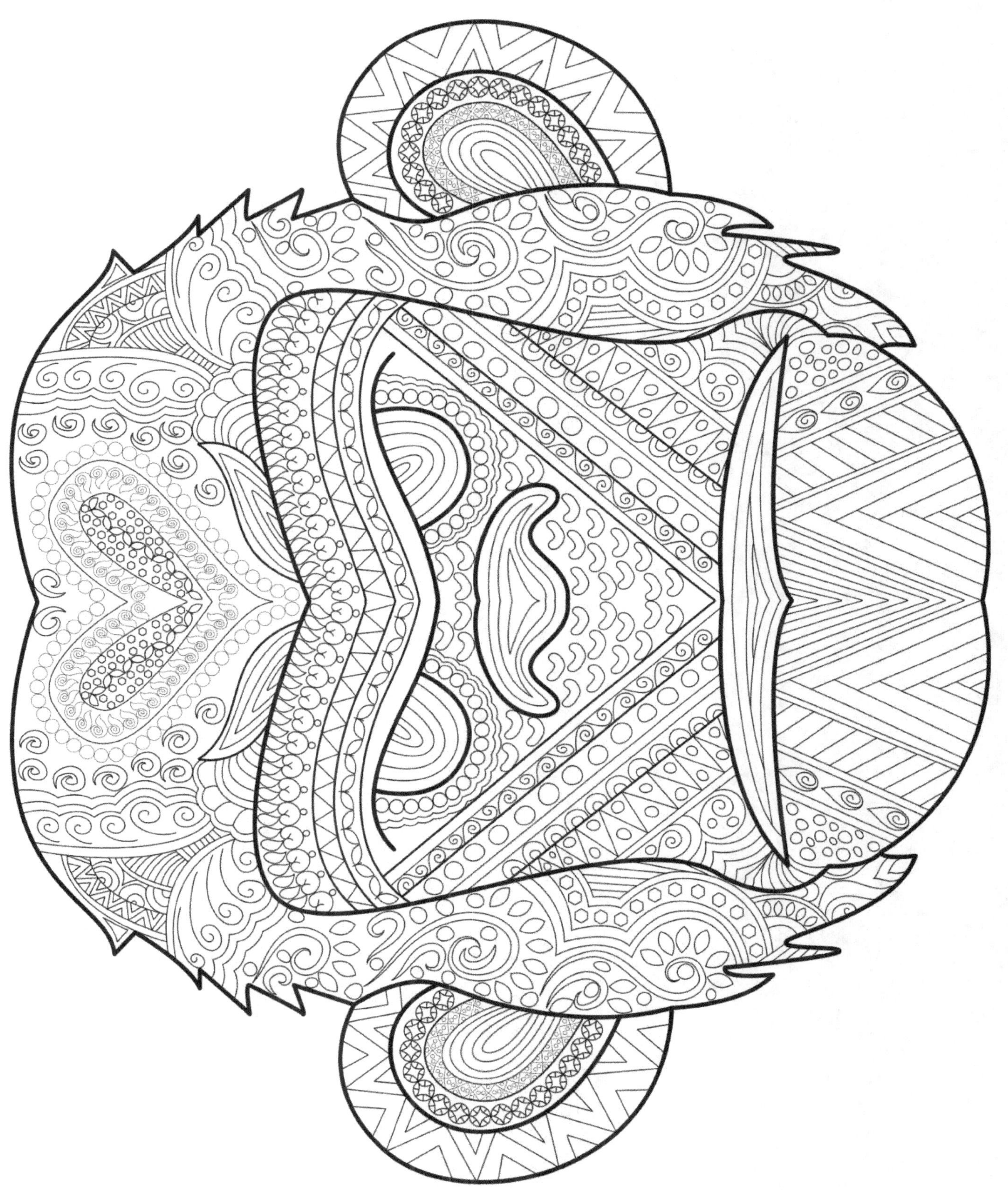

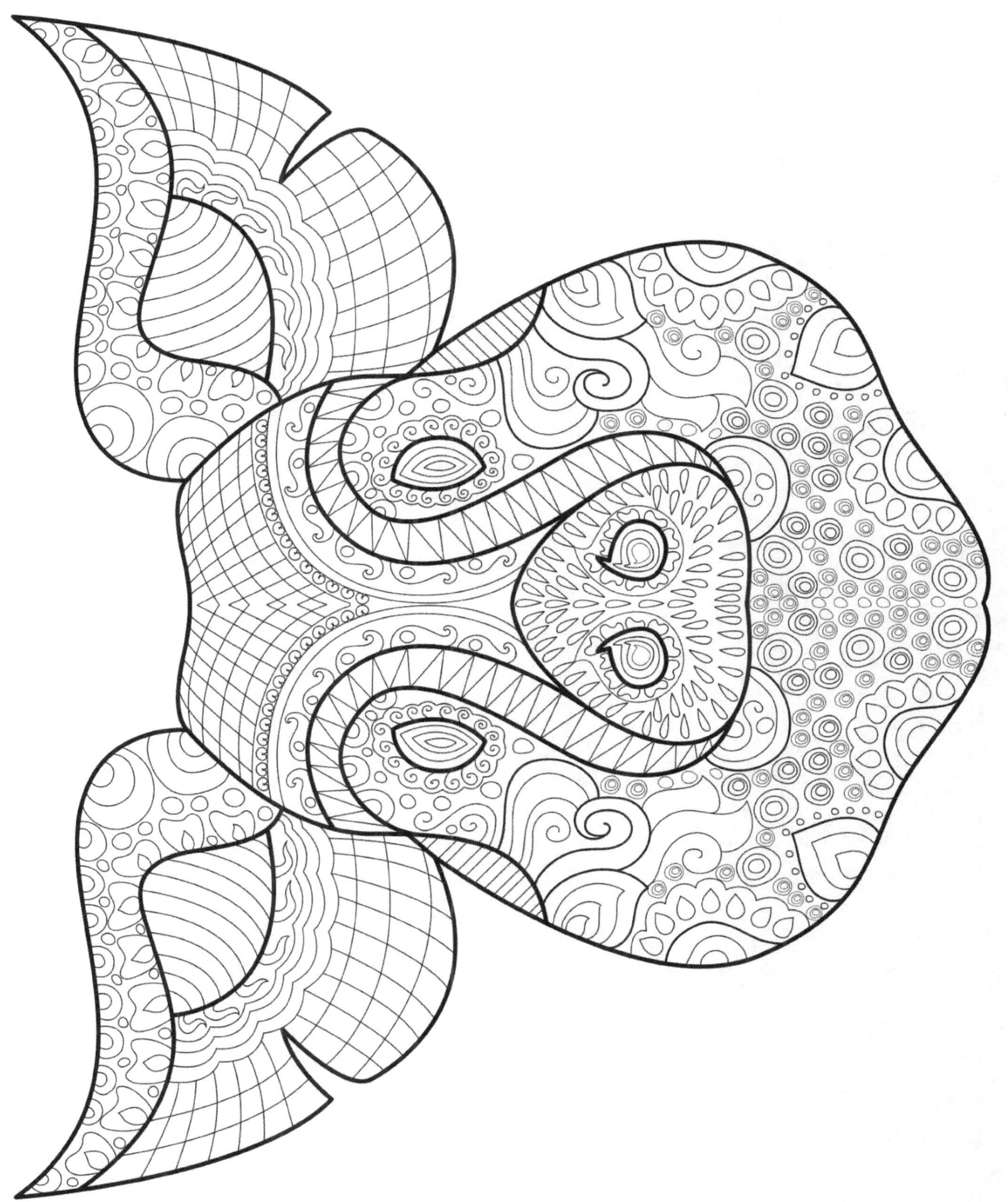

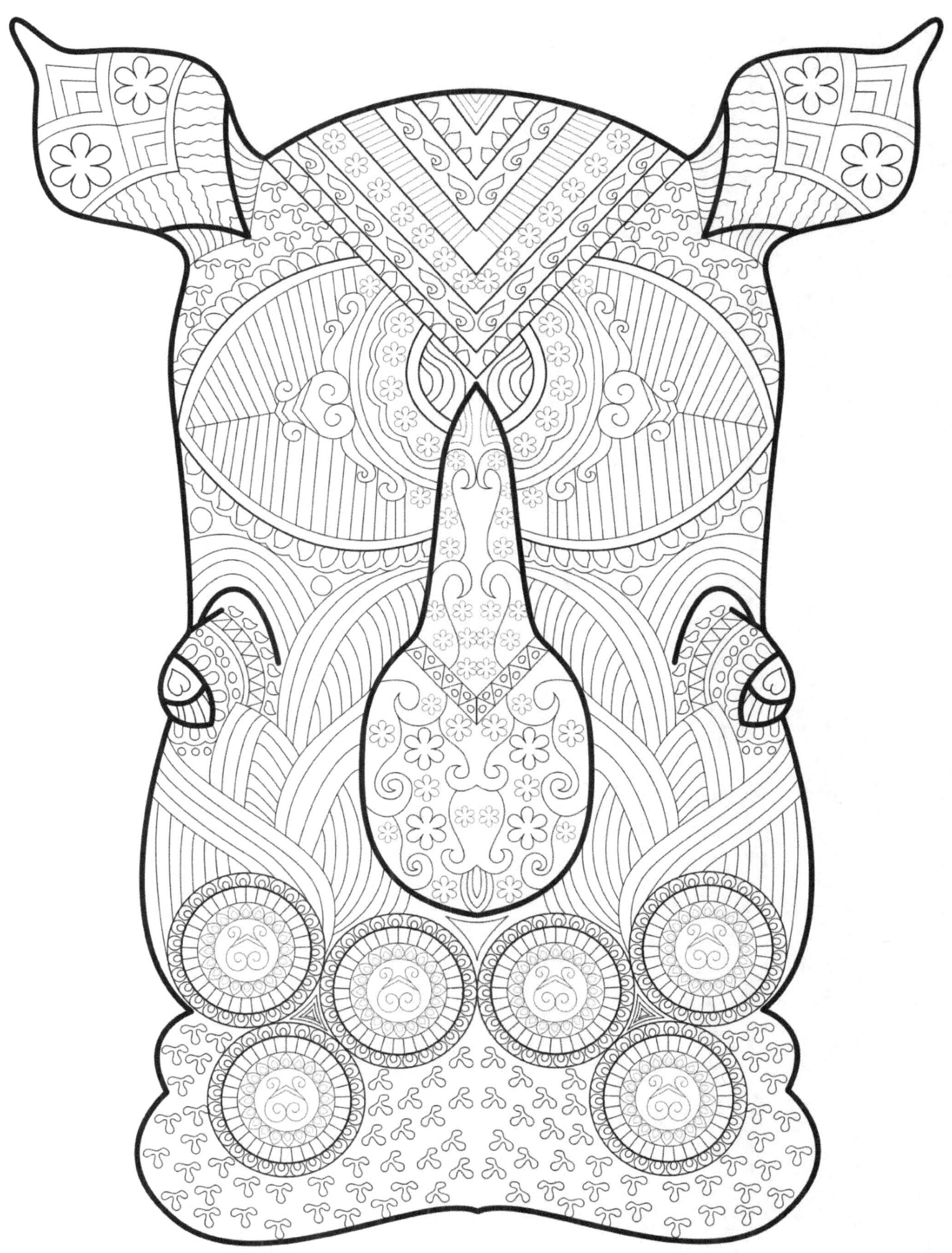

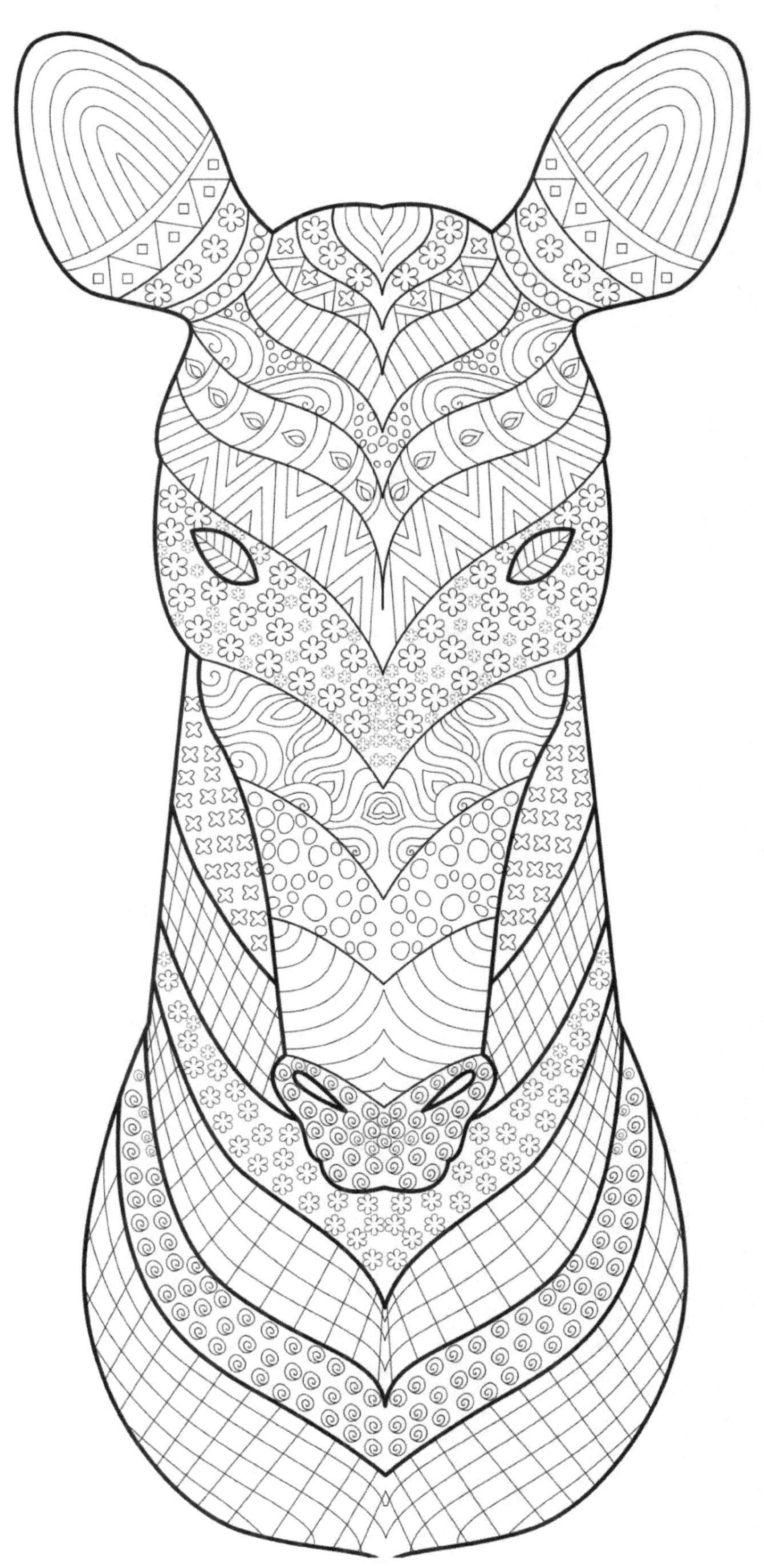